MR. PRESIDENT

TRUMP AND AMERICAN POLITICS

NEELOTPAL SINGH

ISBN 978-1-63832-826-1

To my parents

Contents

Preface

After closely analysing the 4 interesting years of presidency of Donald Trump and going through a thrilling election night of US 2020 Presidential election, I decided to write about Donald Trump.I am writing a book on him it does not mean I am a big supporter of him,but I do find him as an interesting political character,that's why I decided to write about him.Donald Trump's victory was a matter of shock for Pundits. I am writing this book in many volumes,this volume describes Trump's journey from a young businessman to commander in chief,his political thoughts when he was young,his presidential campaign of 2016.It also provides an opportunity to relive the thrill of election night of 2016.

Thank you!

Neelotpal singh

Email-singhneelotpal6000@gmail.com

JOURNEY FROM A BUSINESSMAN TO COMMANDER-IN-CHIEF

I

INTRODUCTION

"TRUMP"-people in America generally equate this word with luxury,wealth or money.

bhhAfter divorce with Ivana he married Marla Maples in 1993. This couple have one daughter Tiffany Trump. But they were divorced in 1999. In 2005 Trump married Melania Knauss(Melania Trump).This couple have a son Barron Trump.

Donald Trump initially began his work at his Father's real estate company.In 1970s Trump started expanding his business under the banner of Trump Organization.

About the nature of Trump many people have many opinions like some consider him arrogant, for some he is a true patriot, for some he is a perfect businessman,for some people he is people's president,for some he is a demagogue and many more interpretations are there.

Although he was a businessman, he was used to comment on foreign and domestic policies of the country and frequently criticised US government policies.

MR. PRESIDENT

II

1980s

In the 1980s,in an interview he was asked what America should be? He answered that "It really should be a country that gets the respect of other countries". Signs of this thought can be seen in his slogan of "America first".In the same interview he criticised the American response to the "Hostage crisis" caused by Iran.

Interestingly, in the same interview he was asked if he would like to be the president of the United States. But he said " I really don't believe that". Further he said " I do not think that somebody with strong views and somebody with kind of views that may be little bit unpopular which may be right but may be unpopular, wouldn't necessarily have a chance of getting elected against somebody with no great brain but a big smile". He also shared his views about the capabilities of the president of the United States, he said "The one proper president can turn this country around".This was the thought process of 34 year old Donald Trump.

In the 1980s Trump became deeply involved in his Real estate business.He became popular in the 1980s due his unique nature.In the 1980s he looked like a politician because he has been commenting on domestic and foreign policies consistently throughout the decade.He criticised the US government in a very harsh manner.

In 1987 He spent a huge amount of money on a full page newspaper ad in which he criticised the foreign policy of then US president.After analysing these things many people started stipulating that Trump might run for presidency,one more thing-In 1987 he was a Republican.

In an interview in 1987 with Larry King, criticising US policies he said" They(other countries of the world) laugh at us..because of our own stupidity".In the same interview he strongly criticised US policies on Japan.

US-Japan- US-Japan relations in the 1970s and 1980s were not smooth. The US called Japan insensitive because Japan was exporting oil from Iran during the Hostage crisis. In the 1980s there was a common perception that Japan was not fulfilling its role as alliance partner.In mid 1980s economic friction between Japan and the United States was at peak.There were strains in US Japan relations due to Contribution of Japan in the first Gulf war.

In the 1980s Trade deficit of the United States with Japan has been consistently increasing.So the relative economic strength of America and Japan was undergoing a significant change, mainly in the 1980s.

The main instance of non cooperation of Japan with America in the 1980s was Japanese opposition to the United States efforts to get Japan to open its market more and more to foreign products and to change other economic policies which were considered against the interests of the United States. Gradually currency of Japan became stronger so Japan was able to purchase more and more goods from American Market and made huge investments in the

United States (After Britain Japan became the second largest investor in America).Due to these reasons Businessman Donald Trump harshly criticizes US policies on Japan.In that interview he argued "Why aren't these countries-these wealthy money machines are paying us for protection of their freedom".

In the early and mid 1970s New York was facing a great economic crisis unemployment rate was spurting. Large number of people left this city and went to some other places.Trump completely Transformed New York city by making Trump Tower etc.In 1982 he said "What's happened is phenomenal I haven't seen anything to the extent that I have seen in New york,It is now from the real-estate point of view probably become the hardest city in the world...(It is due to) the psychology of making new york a winner as opposed to loser." So in the 1970s and early 1980s Trump completely transformed the New york city.He also got the support of the City administration,Trump organisation was given a Tax holiday of 45 million dollars.

Due to these things there was a spurt in employment in New York.More and more people who left New york,at the time of crisis, started returning to this city.New shops and Hotels started mushrooming again.

Again in his 1987 interview he emphasized that he was not going to run for president.He criticised America's expenditure on Japan,Saudi Arabia,Kuwait etc.

In the 1988 Oprah Winfrey show, a lady asked him "what would you do differently(different from other presidents)?" He replied "Forget about enemies,To enemies you can't talk so easily.I will make our allies pay their shares." He criticised US policy on Kuwait he said "people of Kuwait are living like kings still we are paying for them...It's a joke." His attitude towards allies can be traced in his presidential years.

III

1990s and 2000s

1990s was not a good decade for Trump.He had various conflicts with his wife Ivana Trump and finally they divorced in 1992.And he again married with another women.But at the end of the decade he again became single.There were various controversies associated with him in terms of his relations with women.In this decade his business empire was also shaking.In 1990 Trump opened his another Casino hotel in atlantic city "TAJ MAHAL CASINO".But at the the end of 1991 all 3 casinos of atlantic city filled for bankruptcy.In an interview in 1999 he said "Who knows better about hard times than me?" But in the late 1990s he started recovering from the economic crisis that he faced throughout the decade.In 1999 he was about to decide whether he could run for president of the United states.

In the 1990s Trump's real-estate empire was under huge debt. His wife Ivana also left him after news of his affair with Marla Maples, whom he married in 1993.Ivana was demanding $10 million.These were testing times for Donald Trump. In an interview Trump said "That was a terrible, horrible period,All of a sudden you're in this position, when the world is falling around you, and it could take you down."

During this crisis Trump continued pressing the bankers to reduce his debt,because he could not pay.But in front of the public he was completely different. In public he maintained his extravagant,luxurious and ritzy image.It can be seen from this wedding ceremony in 1993.It was a grand ceremony in Trump hotel.After seeing this bankers were astonished..After 6 yearsTrump divorced and again became single.

Trump somehow handled the financial crisis. In his book "The Art of the Comeback," he hailed that time as the "most brilliant period" because he performed under so much stress and huge pressure.He also said in this book - "Ranting and raving, cajoling, always selling, and generally having to be either the nicest person in the world or one of the worst."He started developing his brand.He started using the name "Trump" on everything he possessed.In Trump tower almost everything had word 'Trump' on it

Trump soap,Trump shampoo,Trump coffee mug,Trump sweets,Trump wine glass,Trump football.Gradually 'Brand Trump' became popular.In this way Trump created a 'Trump environment' and he wanted people to frequently think and speak the word "Trump".Gradually he developed his personality as a rockstar.Gradually he developed huge 'Brand capital'.This Brand development helped Trump a lot in handling the financial crisis.This rockstar image also helped him in 2016 Republican primaries and in 2016 presidential election.

Trump said that the financial crisis of the 1990s had a good effect on his children Donald Trump Jr., Ivanka and Eric Trump.They became more strong.It also taught them to stick together. Later in 2016 we saw that they were among the closed advisers of Trump in his election campaign.During this period Trump started aggressive attacks on his critics.For example a stock analyst Marvin Roffman questioned the financial stability of Trump's casino- Taj Mahal in 1990, Trump threatened to sue. Mr. Roffman said "I was attacking his brand and that's something Trump can't allow." This trait also can be seen in the 2016 presidential campaign.

It was 1999, and Donald Trump was almost running for president.In 1999, Trump started thinking that could an extravagant rockstar real estate developer and an author of some self-help books, be the President of The United States?? In 1999, Trump quitted the Republican Party to join the Reform Party and sought the Reform party's presidential nomination.

Supported by Roger Stone he thought to pursue the nomination of the Reform Party. Reform party was founded in 1995.It is a centrist, populist party.It was founded by Ross Perot as an alternative to Republican and Democratic party. Perot got nearly 19 percent of the vote in the 1992 presidential election as an independent candidate.He contested the 1996 election as a candidate of the Reform party and got 8.4 percent vote,which is the highest share of vote for any third party candidate in the USA. It was a remarkable success for him. The Reform Party was not a weak third party. Ross Perot's electoral successes in 1992 and 1996, the party was on all 51 ballots and had money from the Federal Election Commission,these things made it relatively strong. Trump entered the race and gained a huge media attention as an alternative to Pat Buchanan. He won the California Reform Party primary and then he also said that he could run the United States of America.

Once Pat Buchanan argued that Nazi Germany posed no direct threat to the United States.Trump catched this,and he Trump said "Look, he's a Hitler lover. I guess he's an anti-Semite. He doesn't like the blacks, he doesn't like the gays.In this period Trump continued aggressive personal attacks and continued piling huge publicity capital. But In the 2016 elections the same Buchanan praised some of Trump's positions and declared him the favorite to win the Republican nomination.

In the end, Trump quitted the race due to the internal conflicts of the Reform party. So it was just a way to gain more and more publicity, nothing else.He argued that the Reform Party could not provide the "support a candidate needs to win.". He also said, when asked about future prospects of his White House dream-"in a number of years, I might consider it.

But one thing should be remembered: Trump used these campaigns as opportunities to gain more and more publicity, nothing more than that.Because if he really wanted to be the POTUS, he would have chosen Republican ot Democratic party for this. So these were just steps. He was preparing for something big in future ....

In the 2000s he started polishing his personality as a popular leader cum businessman.At that time he was a member of Reform party.Interestingly, In an 2001 interview a reporter said "The president of United States Donald Trump" then trump said "Sounds good".In 2004 he launched a TV show " The Apprentice " which was the most important reason, which made Trump popular among citizens(voters). The famous slogan "You're fired" originated from this show.Trump's popularity was at its peak during this period.He soon married his girlfriend Melania Trump.Again in the 2004 election there were speculations that he might run for presidency.He took cameras with him while going to vote in 2004 presidential elections.But he continued his main work as a real estate developer.He made various new buildings in foreign countries. Those were very beautiful and attractive.In 2000s, he started purchasing golf courses.But in this decade the era of constructing new buildings in New york came to an end and at the end of this decade Trump was completely prepared to enter politics.

IV

2010s

In the early years of 2010s Trump made his first big appearance in politics,when he targeted president Obama' background.He raised the issue of President Obama's Birth Record.But Obama scolded him on this issue.And this issue did not provide any political mileage to Trump.In February 2011 he decided not to run for White House.In the beginning of 2015 Trump said in Iowa: "The last thing we need is another Bush." The real estate developer and TV star Donald Trump launched his presidential campaign on 16 June 2015,ending more than two decades of will-he or won't-he speculation, with the idea of running for the White house.

Trump made his announcement at the Trump Tower(Fifth Avenue,New York) with the campaign slogan, "Make America Great Again(MAGA).He said-"So, ladies and gentlemen, I am officially running for president of the United States, and we are going to make our country great again," Trump delivered a lengthy 45-minute speech related to issues like currency manipulation, China,Iran,terrorism,immigration and job creation.In this speech he also took shots at the president and his competitors on the Republican side. He further said "Sadly the American dream is dead,But if I get elected president I will bring it back bigger and better and stronger than ever before."

Trump described himself as the "most successful person ever to run for the presidency, by far," He pointed out that he owns a "Gucci store that's worth more than Romney." (For your information-Mitt Romney was the Republican nominee for White House in 2012 election and he is an ardent critic of Trump.) So,after listening to his speech it is evident that he made his wealth and success in business a center issue of his presidential campaign. He pointed out that his wealth and successful business career qualified him to be a president. It would also allow him to rid himself of the special interests, that according to him, control American politics.

He said "Our country is in serious trouble. We don't have victories anymore," he said."When was the last time anyone saw us beating, let's say, China in a trade deal?"They kill us. I beat China all the time."In early polls, more than half of Republicans said they had a negative view of him ,which is a tough start for his campaign.Trump expressed his support for gun rights and said he would protect the rights of working people.

Presidential Race of 2016-

Players in the presidential race of 2016-
Democrat-
Hillary Clinton, former First Lady and Secretary of State
Martin O'Malley, former governor of Maryland
Bernie Sanders, independent senator from Vermont

Lincoln Chafee, governor of Rhode Island
Republican-
Donald Trump
Jeb Bush, former Florida Governor
Ted Cruz, Texas senator
Rick Santorum,
Marco Rubio, Florida senator since 2011
George Pataki, former three-term governor of New York
Ben Carson, author and neurosurgeon
Carly Fiorina
Mike Huckabee, former governor of Arkansas
Rand Paul, Kentucky senator
Lindsey Graham, South Carolina senator since 2003
Rick Perry, former Texas governor

Trump 2016 campaign

After Donald Trump announced his candidacy for the presidential election,many people laughed at him.For many people he was a cartoon character.After his announcement in June 2015 Donald Trump started an aggressive campaign for Primaries.(**Primaries-**In US to get the nomination for the presidential election, candidates of a particular party compete in a election and the person who wins this election gets the nomination from that party.) traveled to many primary states like New Hampshire Iowa to campaign.In Iowa he was interviewed by a Republican pollstar.In that interview his remarks on John Mccain,created controversy.This was the beginning of series of controversies related to politician Trump. This controversy became very dangerous for the novice trump campaign.But Trump absorbed this shock.After that he went to the West, where he held various rallies and in Las Vegas and Los

Angeles.In July 2015 he went to the Mexican border,Texas.

On August 6, 2015,in Cleveland, the first Republican primary debate took place on Fox News.Here he had to debate with group of Republicans who were hailed as best in the generation.Interestingly, he said,inter alia, "I can totally make that pledge that if I am the nominee,I pledge I will not run as an independent."So in a very meandering way he kept alive the speculations of "Third Party".But in September 2015, Trump ended these speculations when he signed a pledge promising his allegiance to the Republican Party.After that debate he again created controversy which was related to his comments about Megyn Kelly.(Meghan Kelly was one of the moderators for the the first Republican primary debate and she asked tough questions to Trump.),which were perceived as dirty and disgusting by many.At that time Meghan Kelly was star on Fox news.Trump used this controversy,because his supporters like his anti-establishment agenda. Trump and Steve Bannon(Breitbart.com) launched a camapign against Meghan Kelly and soon Trump supporters flooded Twitter with millions of harsh Tweets against Meghan.All these things were just for 'one primary debate question' .Meanwhile, Trump travelled throughout the country and continued campaigning very hard.He launched a very provocative and enthusiastic campaign. People involved in the Trump campaign decided to "let Trump be Trump".

As far as the rallies are concerned, Trump, as a good producer(of the show "The Apprentice"),made sure that the staging and extravaganza was perfect.In his rallies he used to create a different euphoria among the people involved in the rally.He always tried to put forward something new and interesting .Once he said "Everytime I speak they put me on live television,So every time I have to make different speeches these guys go around make similar speeches hundreds and hundreds and hundreds of time".People want to see him angry,uncensored,unfiltered.He used slogan like "America First","Build That Wall", "Lock Her Up","CNNSucks","Drain the swamp".Various people interpreted his chantings differently his critics called them as fear mongering his supporters called it as Truth telling.After a series of rallies and his vigorous campaign he started winning primary elections in many states.He created tensions among his opponents,establishment suddenly woke up against him and they started taking him seriously.Because now establishment knew that this Trump movement,which was an anti-establishment,populist movement, can shook their own foundations.

Both republican and democrat establishments went after him.Republicans like Lindady Graham, Marco Rubio,Mitt Romney, Ted Cruz etc. criticised him harshly. Another Republican debate took place in The peace centre, South Carolina,he again tried to assert himself strongly.He destroyed every republican leader on the stage..He made funny, interesting,unconventional comments.(Like he called Marco Rubio "a little guy".) because he knew that people love entertainment. Now, after seeing the direction of political wind, his republican opponents started quitting the race. Gradually,tension was increasing in his rallies,we have seen many skirmishes in his rallies.Trump made this election a crusade.

Till July 2016 he defeated the Rublican establishment.He became bigger than Republican party itself.Now he became the centre of Republican Party.In July 2016,He became the GOP(GOP is the another name of Republican party) nominee of the presidential election of 2016.He said in GOP convention"Nobody knows the system better than me,Which is why I alone can fix it". A few days later Hillary Clinton became Democrate nominee.

V
Trump vs Hillary Clinton

Let us talk about Hillary clinton-

On 12 April 2015 she announced that she was also running for the president of the United States.Hillary Clinton came into the spotlight during the presidential campaign of his husband Bill clinton,then governor of Arkansas,in 1990-1991. After Bill clinton defeated George H.W. Bush, who was contesting election for his second term, Hillary Clinton became the FLOTUS(First lady Of The United States).

She was a very active first lady,an ardent advocate of women issues and child care.After 8 long years as FLOTUS she decided to run for the senate from New York.She won that senate race and became the first lady to win an elective office in United States.So it was the beginning of career of politician Hillary Clinton. She also won a second term in the Senate in 2006 by a huge margin.Clinton unleashed her first presidential campaign in January 2007. But in Democratic primaries she was defeated by Barack Obama.

She conceded by saying "Although we were not able to shatter that highest and hardest glass ceiling this time, thanks to you it has 18 million cracks in it."

After winning the 2008 election Obama decided to make her Secretary of State. During her tenure Hillary Clinton used a private email server to conduct official works, which created controversy and fierce opposition by other lawmakers. This issue was also exploited by Trump during the 2016 presidential campaign.Hillary Clinton again decided to run for president in 2015.Hillary clinton won the closely contested Democratic primaries and formally received the Democratic Party's presidential nomination on July 26, 2016. Like in 2000, she again created history because by accepting her nomination, she became the first woman to be nominated for president of the United States by a major political party.

Hillary Clinton generally took liberal position on various social issues, she supported abortion rights, marriage equality etc. She supported capital punishment in federal jurisdictions for very limited purpose.One of the most important issues in US politics is immigration, democrats encourage it so she also supported immigration reforms. She also decided to repeal gun industry liability protections and implement comprehensive regulations. She said that she would increase taxes on the top 1 percent of earners, leaving tax rates the same for taxpayers with smaller incomes. Clinton said she believed in "American exceptionalism" and advocated for the U.S. to act as a leader in world affairs.

Let us see trump's position on various issues-

As I mentioned, immigration is the most important issue in American politics.Trump's domestic politics focused heavily on immigration and deregulating the environmental regulations. He proposed strengthening U.S. immigration laws. He promised for the construction of a wall along the U.S.-Mexico border,and according to him the costs of which Mexican government will cover. Trump called climate change a "hoax". He also talked about repealing the Affordable Care Act, or Obamacare. Trump decided to nominate conservative judges. He opposed abortion and once suggested that women who have abortions should be punished but he also said that there should be exceptions in the case of rape, incest, and risks to the mother's life.

Trump supported cutting taxes at all levels. He was an ardent champion of protectionism, his opposition to international free-trade deals was an important feature of his campaign. His tax proposals included cuts at all income levels, an end to the estate tax, and a tax deduction for childcare expenses. He called international trade like NAFTA(North American Free Trade Area) and TPP(Trans pacific partnership) -"a disaster" and supported increased tariffs on imports and advocated protectionism.Trump supported raising the minimum wage to $10 an hour.

Trump promoted his "America First" agenda to foreign policy. His main target were allies.This approach involved potentially reshaping U.S. commitments to NATO countries and other allies. He also decided to reshape the US relations with UN,WTO,WHO etc. It can be seen from his statements in 1980s, he was very critical to his allies also.He always wanted them pay their share.He adopted a more aggressive foreign policy in the fight against the Islamic State and in the war on terror.Trump called for a ban on Muslims entering the country from nations with "a history of exporting terrorism," he criticized the Iran deal,JCPOA, calling it a "bad deal." Trump also decided to improve U.S.

relations with Russia in the fight against the Islamic State.

Hillary tried to exploit the issues of racism,diversity,Muslims,Xenophobia etc.So democrates called Mr.khan,who was father of a great Muslim American martyr, in the democratic convention. He criticised Mr.Trump a lot. It created a different environment in democratic convention.Everyone became emotional.So again this was another challenge for Donald Trump.Trump,suffering with his habit of not letting anything just go away,responded and attacked Mr.khan many times.This led to the eruption of a huge controversy. Trump's Poll numbers declined.Nearly 80 days before the election, Trump shook up his campaign and brought in Steve Bannon, the chairman of the right-wing website Breitbart.According to Roger stone,Trump's Political Adviser,- "Bannon is a bomb thrower. Bannon joins the campaign because Bannon has a superior knowledge of alternative media, combined with the fact that he is kind of a swashbuckler and a revolutionary, a guy who can think outside the box". With the help of Bannon and various new advisers Trump made his position strong again.

First presidential debate-On 26 September 2016,Trump and Clinton are ready to collide,in one of the most interesting political showdown.This was the most watched debate in American history.As we know that Trump generally does not prefer to prepare.He always relies on his instincts and he prepares his content instantly.This is also a very different quality of Trump. So,He mocked Clinton for spending so much of her time preparing for the debate.According to a Republican Pollster, Frank Luntz-" Arguably, he was the worst-prepared candidate in the history of American politics when he stepped up against Hillary Clinton for that first debate, and it showed."

After this another bomb was thrown on Trump campaign,this time a big one- Just two days before the second debate, an un-aired video from the TV show Access Hollywood.According to Mark Fischer, Co-Author, Trump Revealed- "There was one account after another about Donald Trump attacking women, groping women, saying nasty things about women. But the moment that counts is the moment this is on video."In that video he was making disgusting and crude jokes.This allegation was so powerful that even people of his campaign were unable to defend this.Everyone from his campaign became silent. It was a disaster for the Trump campaign.Many people thought his candidacy was over.

According to Corey Lewandowski, Former Trump Campaign Manager-This was the October surprise, had the ability to take down a campaign. And the internal discussion amongst the campaign, some were "You need to apologize immediately," and some were "You need to double down."

According to Katy Tur-"I think with the exception of maybe one or two people, everyone thought that that was the end. How do you survive this? How do you survive this? As a Republican, how do you survive advocating or saying you're allowed to grab women in their private parts because you're a star? That is just not something that anybody can survive."

Now every single person in the United States of America was looking towards Trump,because it was the climax of the series of controversies related to Trump. This allegation was so powerful that it forced Trump, who never apologized for any wrong acts or comments, to come out and to apologize(in his unique style,means apology cum attack).

He came out on TV and said "I've never said I'm a perfect person, nor pretended to be someone that I'm not. I've said and done things I regret, and the words released today on this more than a decade-old video are one of them....Bill Clinton has actually abused women, and Hillary has bullied, attacked, shamed and intimidated his victims...We will discuss this more in the coming days. See you(Hillary) at the debate on Saturday."

To know the state of mind of Trump,which was surprising, have a look at his reply to Robert Costa of The Washington Post- "Costa, I've lived life. I've seen so much in my life, business, personal. This is nothing. I've survived everything else. I'm going to survive this....There's no chance I quit,Not one chance. I am in this to the end."

Trump again absorbed the shock of another bomb,now headed towards the second presidential debate.But Trump wanted to write the climax in his own way, like a good TV star. So just before second presidential debate,Trump also launched a missile from his arsenal-Without any prior information,he came up with a press conference with all Bill Clinton's accusers,women who had accused Bill and Hillary Clinton of various bad works....The man who engineered this surprise was the "Bomb-thrower," according to Roger Stone, Steve Banon.

Again everyone was shocked.No one had expected anything like that.

Second presidential debate-In this debate Trump was aggressively attacking on Hillary Clinton.He said-"If I win, I am going to instruct my attorney general to get a special prosecutor to look into your situation because there has never been so many lies, so much deception. There has never been anything like it." Let me tell a tiny part of that that debate to show the heat of that debate-

HILLARY CLINTON: It's just awfully good that someone with the temperament of donald trump is not in charge of law in our country

DONALD TRUMP: Because you'd be in jail.

Elecrion is getting closer. Trump continues launching slogans like "Drain the swamp" etc. and continues promoting his anti establishment agenda.Suddenly, Wikileaks comes into the picture.It is said that Wikileaks is about to release significant material related to Hillary Clinton.Thousands of private e-mails,many of them embarrassing,from Clinton campaign chairman John Podesta were released.Like Access Hollywood was for Trump, it was a disaster for Clinton campaign,But because they did not have a TV star like Trump, they got impacted badly, by this event.Now Trump became more charged.He became more offensive.See how happy he was-On this matter he said- "Wikileaks is amazing, the stuff that's coming out. It shows she's a real liar!

........This Wikileaks stuff is unbelievable! It tells you the inner heart. You got to read it.

................Wikileaks! I love WikiLeaks!"

But there were many allegations of Russian collusion in this matter.

According to David Sanger- "It was cyber mixed with information warfare. And the press, The New York Times included, became the handmaiden to the process because these emails couldn't be ignored as news. They were newsy. They were out there. It's not like you could ignore it and not write about it. But in writing about it, you're doing the work that Vladimir Putin had in mind."Another blow to the Cinton campaign was that the FBI director, James Comey,decided to resume an investigation of Clinton's personal email server.Now Donald Trump dominated the arena.

Trump exploited each and every allegation against Hillary Clinton.Trump traveled throughout the country building on that momentum and asserting his claims against Clinton. Now for the first time the weight of scandals was more on Clinton's side.

VI
2016 thrilling election night

Clinton or Trump?

8/11/2016 -Decision day came-The one of the most consequential presidentials race was about to end. Who will be the winner? Each and every one of the citizens of America and every head of state was excited for the answer of this question.

There was a nail-biting race between Trump and Clinton.It was one of the most remarkable political nights in modern history.As night gets darker,race becomes more interesting.Steve Kornacki,in his khakis, was making the race more interesting. Every news channel on the globe was talking about this. Everyone was guessing about who is going to win?

From Khamenei to Putin,from Kim Jong Un to Xinping, every head of state was excited about the result.Every international organisation like NATO,UN,WHO,WTO was uncertain and anxious about their future.Every political analyst,reporter,pollster,sociologist was trying to philosophise the situation through various philosophical phrases and was trying to make the night memorable.

Crowd gathered as count continues,everyone was focused on the swing states.Florida was the must win state for Trump.Gradually people started thinking that it looks like much better night for Donald Trump than expected,when news channels started saying-

.................Trump wins Ohio,a very important swing state.

.................Trump wins North Carolina.

.................Trump wins Florida, a must win state.

.................Trump wins Iowa.

.................Trump wins Wisconsin.

and

.................Trump wins Pennsylvania

.................**Trump wins the 2016 presidential election.**

In his victory speech he said-"The forgotten men and women of our country will be forgotten no longer"

So on 8 nov 2016 he cashed in all his Financial as well as celebrity capital. Trump defied all conventional wisdom,all big pollsters,political pundits,nearly every journalist,whole establishment.Everyone was stunned.What started as impossible is now a reality.This was an election of lifetime. First time ever in the history of the United States,a person who never held or even ran for a political office and has zero experience in the military,is elected as commander in chief of the US.Everyone was crying, some due to sadness and others due to immense happiness.On 20 January 2017 with the chanting of oath- "I Donald John Trump.............,So help me god."-America got its new Commander in chief Donald J. Trump.

VII

REASONS FOR THIS UNPRECEDENTED CHANGE

Let us look at some of the facts that catalysed this unprecedented change.First of all Trump's anti-establishment image is the most powerful thing for which people like him.The most common thing we hear from Trump's supporters is "He is not a politician..".Because people became frustrated with establishment politician.

One thing we have to understand that democratic citizens are very impatient now they do not want to wait much they want a continuous public discourse, they did not want a boring liberal democracy, they want immediate answer of their questions, they want political arguments, but traditional politicians, liberal elites, ruling technocrats are failed to fulfil the demands of common people effectively, so these people get frustrated, sometimes ruling elites in contemporary democracies start believing that masses are incompetent, not hard working, useless, it further increases the anger of common people ,and this anger and frustration is being exploited by Trump and other populist leaders .Because he is an excellent speaker and good attention grabber.He was a reality TV star,a business mogul.He is well versed in attracting people.

Trump biographer Gwenda Blair said: "It gave him 10 years of being in front of the American public being the boss, being CEO, hiring people, famously firing people, being the guy who can fix it, the one who knows everything, being the big authoritarian patriarchal guy." For a decade he projected himself as a boss with the power to say openly- "You're fired!"

Another important thing that people like about him is his anti-establishment agenda.He targeted his own party establishment. Trump launched war on his own party. During and after primaries, he attacked the Bush family, Mitt Romney and John McCain ,House speaker Paul Ryan etc. But many Trump supporters also supported his attacks on the party establishment. They complained that the members of Congress they elected made promises they failed to keep. His supporters were frustrated with the government shutdowns etc. So when Mitt Romney and other establishment leaders criticised Trump ,it actually worked to his advantage.

His opponent Hillary Clinton as wife of a former president Bill Clinton, two times senator and secretary of state, she was the ultimate face of the establishment.And Trump had started a rigorous movement against establishment.So it shook the very foundation of Hillary Clinton's campaign.According to Robin Tolmach Lakoff-"The 2016 election was persistently viewed as having as its theme Change vs. the Status Quo, with Trump representing the former. But in fact Clinton was the true "change" candidate: had she been elected, our perceptions of the permissible relationship between gender and power, in existence since we became Homo sapiens if not before, would have had to change. That would have been (as is now all too clear) intolerable to too many Americans."

According to Trump supporters he would give them jobs,he would MAKE AMERICA GREAT AGAIN(MAGA) He would bring a perfect system. According to Thomas Anthony Lynch-"Trump's election represents a developmental progression of America's electoral system from a political process to an entertainment process."

Thomas Anthony Lynch also described the history of the media in presidential elections. The term 'political star' references the image of a politician who is media friendly and well known to the public via magazine articles, newspaper interviews, television programmes and other media images. Through these media resources, a 'star candidate' either resonates or not with the public. The first US presidential election in which traditional media such as print and radio and the newer medium of television played an important role was the 1960 presidential campaign between Kennedy and Nixon.Since the time of Kennedy's 1960 victory, the how well presidential candidates played on television became crucial for success,Gradually Many movie stars started entering into politics,like California governor Ronald Reagan and later American president Clint Eastwood as mayor of Carmel in California, Ronald Reagan later American president, Jesse Ventura as governor of Minnesota, Al Franken as Minnesota senator.But I think Important thing in Trump is that he was TV star and a successful businessman both, which makes him different from many of the previous movie stars turned politicians.Trump always uses songs etc. to set the stage and a very good environment.He makes his rallies entertaining.

Trump's speech- Trump's speech also makes him different from establishment politicians.Trump uses broken sentences with utmost clarity.Many journalists and political scientists called it a sign of a disordered mind.But for his supporters it is a good thing.

Trump tries to exaggerate his arguments using words like "really","Enormously" ,"by far", "very,very" etc. .He repeats a sentence or phrase, many times to prove that phrase, true.Trump never apologize or defend any accusations on him he just spins them.Trump is famous for slogans like "Make America great again", "Build the wall", "Drain the swamp" etc.

He always asserted his success as a businessman and TV star.In this way he tried to assert that he was the only legitimate person in the 2016 election to be elected as the president.Through his speeches people understand Trump at an emotional level. When he spoke, his audience was able to finish his sentences.In 2016 campaign he invoked the fear of unemployment, worries about the United States losing its status as superpower,concerns related to immigration etc. Trump validated the fear and concerns (which were created,mainly,by Trump himself) of his supporters and justified their anger.Because of this this many people called him fear mongerer.

So Trump is the ultimate face of politainment. He was well versed in political communication. He has a very powerful position in the politico-media complex. The US media is also obsessed with him,because Trump is an instrument of ratings for TV channels.So if they want very good ratings they have to show every activity of Trump.It made him more popular. Trump also exploited this quality of media.He always said something new,controversial but the things which resonated with his voters.

The bottom line is that- it is still a matter of research how a person with zero experience in politics or military,in spite of opposition of print and electronic media,opposition of members of his own party,opposition of almost every intellectual,various serious allegations etc. won the 2016 US presidential elections.

Thank You!